THE PRAYERS
of JANE AUSTEN

Introduction & Commentary
by Terry Glaspey

HARVEST HOUSE PUBLISHERS
EUGENE, OREGON

THE PRAYERS *of* JANE AUSTEN

Text copyright © 2015 by Terry Glaspey

Published by Harvest House Publishers
Eugene, Oregon 97402
www.harvesthousepublishers.com

ISBN 978-0-7369-6518-7

Design and production by
Dugan Design Group, Bloomington, Minnesota

Scripture verses are taken from the King James Version of the Bible

All images in this book were found in the British Library's collections, are believed to be in the public domain, and can be viewed at www.bl.uk.

Printed in China.

22 / RDS / 10 9 8 7 6

Introduction

THOUGH JANE AUSTEN WROTE her novels in the early nineteenth century, she continues to be one of the most popular writers of our time. Her wise and witty observations of love and romance, class conflict, and the nature of true virtue and character are as relevant today as when they were first penned.

Her fans enthusiastically read and reread her novels, enjoying every clever turn of phrase and each memorable characterization. In the last twenty years, there has been a renewed interest in Jane, which shows no signs of letting up. Her novels have been turned into popular and award-winning films and TV miniseries, and shelves full of books written by imitators have explored the further adventures of her beloved characters. Jane Austen is truly a unique literary phenomenon.

That she was a distinctly gifted writer is widely known. What is not so commonly known is that Jane was also a woman who embraced the Christian faith wholeheartedly. Her faith was the foundation for her deep understanding of human frailty and folly and the power of true love. Although many biographers have downplayed the faith aspect of her life, the unprejudiced reader finds it abundantly clear that she was a Christian writer. As the daughter of an Anglican pastor, Jane lived a life surrounded by belief in Christ. Though her novels steer clear of any sort of preaching, a morality rooted in faith is found on every page.

But even Jane's most devoted readers are likely unaware of a small collection of prayers she composed. They've been long neglected but have now been brought to light. These prayers have a beautiful formal style, reminiscent of the cadences of the *Book of Common Prayer* with which she was very familiar. She most likely wrote them to use during evening prayer times with her family. Readers who know Jane's novels will recognize her unique voice in these little gems of heartfelt devotion.

These prayers give us a privileged glimpse into Jane's soul. In them she asks God for help and forgiveness as she searches her soul's dark nooks and crannies and examines her attitudes and actions. She expresses deep gratitude to God as well as her heart of trust and surrender to His will. She recognizes "the importance of every day, and every hour as it passes" and asks for God's help to "earnestly strive to make a better use of what Thy goodness may yet bestow on us, than we have done of the time past." These prayers are a small treasure she left behind for those who share in her faith. Reading these prayers—and praying them with her—I hope you'll get a fresh appreciation for the unexpected spiritual depth of this remarkable woman. ❧

THE PRAYERS
of JANE AUSTEN

Jane's three surviving prayers flow
over the following pages. Their
original order and wording have
been retained, and nothing has
been added or subtracted. Each of
the prayers was intended to end
with a recitation of the Lord's
Prayer, but to avoid repetition, the
Lord's Prayer has been added only
at the conclusion of the last
of the three prayers.

I

*G*ive us grace, Almighty Father, so to pray, as to deserve to be heard, to address Thee with our hearts, as with our lips. Thou art everywhere present, from Thee no secret can be hid. May the knowledge of this, teach us to fix our thoughts on Thee, with reverence and devotion that we pray not in vain.

$\mathcal{L}$ook with mercy
on the sins we have
this day committed, and
in mercy make us
feel them deeply, that our
repentance may be sincere,
and our resolutions
steadfast of endeavoring
against the commission of
such in future.

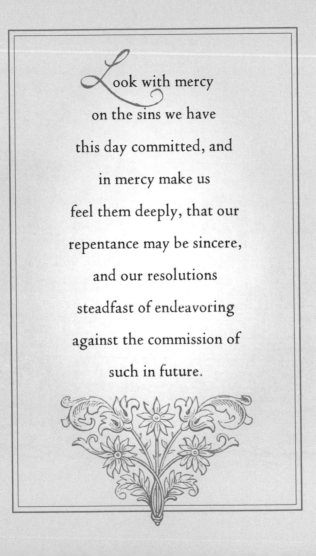

Teach us to
understand the
sinfulness of our own hearts,
and bring to our knowledge
every fault of temper and every
evil habit in which we have
indulged to the discomfort
of our fellow-creatures,
and the danger of
our own souls.

13

May we now, and on each return of night, consider how the past day has been spent by us, what have been our prevailing thoughts, words, and actions during it, and how far we can acquit ourselves of evil.

Have we thought irreverently of Thee, have we disobeyed Thy commandments, have we neglected any known duty, or willingly given pain to any human being? Incline us to ask our hearts these questions, O God, and save us from deceiving ourselves by pride or vanity.

*G*ive us a
thankful sense
of the blessings
in which we live, of the
many comforts of our
lot; that we may not
deserve to lose them
by discontent or
indifference.

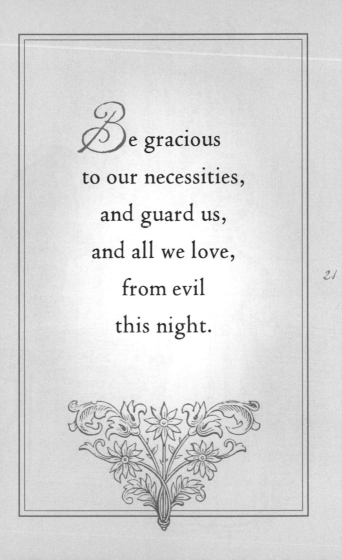

$\mathcal{B}$e gracious
to our necessities,
and guard us,
and all we love,
from evil
this night.

May the sick and afflicted, be now, and ever in Thy care; and heartily do we pray for the safety of all that travel by land or by sea, for the comfort and protection of the orphan and the widow and that Thy pity may be shown upon all captives and prisoners.

23

Above all other blessings,
O God, for ourselves, and for our
fellow-creatures, we implore Thee
to quicken our sense of Thy mercy
in the redemption of the world, of
the value of that holy religion in
which we have been brought up,
that we may not, by our own neglect,
throw away the salvation Thou hast
given us, nor be Christians only
in name. Hear us, Almighty God,
for His sake who redeemed us, and
taught us thus to pray.

II

Almighty God, look down with mercy on Thy servants here assembled and accept the petitions now offered up unto Thee. Pardon, O God, the offenses of the past day. We are conscious of many frailties; we remember with shame and contrition, many evil thoughts and neglected duties; and we have perhaps sinned against Thee and against our fellow-creatures in many instances of which we have no remembrance.

Pardon, O God,
whatever Thou has seen
amiss in us, and give us a
stronger desire of resisting
every evil inclination
and weakening every
habit of sin. Thou knowest
the infirmity of our
nature, and the temptations
which surround us.

Be Thou merciful, O Heavenly Father, to creatures so formed and situated. We bless Thee for every comfort of our past and present existence, for our health of body and of mind and for every other source of happiness which Thou hast bountifully bestowed on us and with which we close this day, imploring their continuance from Thy Fatherly goodness, with a more grateful sense of them, than they have hitherto excited.

$\mathcal{M}$ay the comforts of
every day, be
thankfully felt by us,
may they prompt a
willing obedience of
Thy commandments
and a benevolent spirit
toward every
fellow-creature.

Have mercy, O gracious
Father, upon all that are now
suffering from whatsoever
cause, that are in any
circumstance of danger or
distress. Give them patience
under every affliction,
strengthen, comfort, and
relieve them.

To Thy goodness
we commend ourselves
this night
beseeching Thy protection
of us through its

darkness and dangers.
We are helpless and
dependent; graciously
preserve us.

For all whom we love
and value, for every
friend and connection,
we equally pray;
however divided and
far asunder, we know
that we are alike before
Thee, and under
Thine eye.

May we be
equally united in
Thy faith and fear,
in fervent devotion
towards Thee,
and in Thy merciful
protection
this night.

Pardon, O Lord,

the imperfections of

these our prayers,

and accept them through

the mediation of our

Blessed Saviour,

in whose holy words,

we further address Thee.

III

Father of Heaven,
whose goodness has brought
us in safety to the
close of this day, dispose
our hearts in fervent
prayer. Another day
is now gone, and added
to those, for which we were
before accountable.

Teach us, Almighty
Father, to consider this
solemn truth, as we should do,
that we may feel the importance
of every day, and every hour
as it passes, and earnestly strive
to make a better use of what
Thy goodness may yet bestow on
us, than we have done of
the time past.

*G*ive us grace to endeavor
after a truly Christian spirit
to seek to attain that temper
of forbearance and patience
of which our Blessed Saviour
has set us the highest example;
and which, while it prepares us
for the spiritual happiness of
the life to come, will secure to
us the best enjoyment of what
this world can give.

Incline us, O God,

to think humbly of ourselves,

to be severe only in the

examination of our own conduct,

to consider our fellow-creatures

with kindness, and to judge of

all they say and do with that

charity which we would desire

from them ourselves.

$\mathcal{W}$e thank Thee
with all our hearts for
every gracious dispensation,
for all the blessings
that have attended to our
lives, for every hour
of safety, health, and peace,
of domestic comfort and
innocent enjoyment.

We feel that we
have been blessed far
beyond any thing that we have
deserved; and though we cannot
but pray for a continuance of all
these mercies, we acknowledge
our unworthiness of
them and implore Thee
to pardon the presumption
of our desires.

59

*K*eep us,
O Heavenly Father,
from evil this night. Bring us
in safety to the beginning
of another day and grant
that we may rise again with
every serious and religious
feeling which now
directs us.

May Thy mercy
be extended over
all mankind,
bringing the ignorant
to the knowledge of
Thy truth, awakening
the impenitent,
touching the
hardened.

*L*ook with
compassion upon the
afflicted of every
condition, assuage
the pangs of disease,
comfort the broken
in spirit.

More particularly do we pray for the safety and welfare of our own family and friends wheresoever dispersed, beseeching Thee to avert from them all material and lasting evil of body or mind; and may we by the assistance of Thy Holy Spirit so conduct ourselves on earth as to secure an eternity of happiness with each other in Thy Heavenly Kingdom. Grant this, most Merciful Father, for the sake of our Blessed Saviour in whose holy name and words we further address Thee.

Our Father,
which art in Heaven,
hallowed be
Thy name.
Thy Kingdom come.
Thy will be done
in earth, as
it is in Heaven.

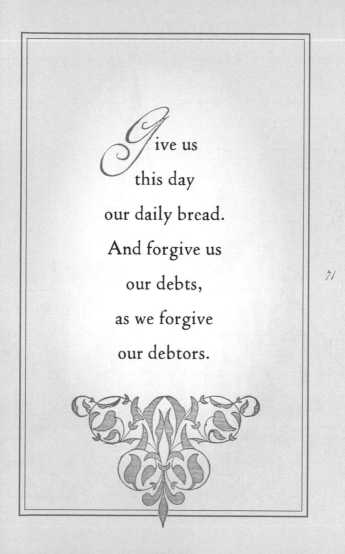

*G*ive us
this day
our daily bread.
And forgive us
our debts,
as we forgive
our debtors.

And lead us not
into temptation,
but deliver us from evil.
For Thine is the
Kingdom, and the power,
and the glory,
forever. Amen.

Jane Austen

WIT, WISDOM, AND FAITH

As you meditate on these beautiful, heartfelt prayers, you realize that you are praying alongside a woman of rare spiritual honesty and depth. To those who have only known Jane Austen for her witty and insightful novels, this might come as a bit of a surprise. But I think these prayers help us understand that there is a deep and abiding faith that upholds the wit and wisdom we find in Jane Austen's probing insights into human nature and human relationships.

Her novels were never intended to be any sort of religious propaganda, and in her letters we find her expressing impatience with those who wear their faith on their sleeves or try to coerce others toward belief by the use of emotional appeals. For Jane, to be a Christian was more about how you lived your life than what you happened to preach. "It isn't what we say or think that defines us," she wrote, "but what we do." So, in her novels we see moral and spiritual truths being lived out in ways that inspire and challenge us.

Jane Austen was born in 1775, the daughter of the rector of a small English parish. Unlike her books, her day-to-day existence would not have provided much fodder for a television miniseries, for she lived an outwardly uneventful life. Never married, she spent her time writing and caring for her family, including her nieces and nephews with whom she was a great favorite. She wrote her books mainly for the sheer pleasure of it, concealing her work under the cover of anonymity. Until late in her writing career, no one outside her family knew her as the author of these remarkable novels. Even with her own family, she was reticent about drawing attention to her creative work. When someone entered the room while she was writing, she would gently slip her manuscript underneath the other papers on her writing desk. She seems to have had little desire for fame and recognition and was content with her quiet domestic life.

Jane began writing when she was very young, and those early compositions show that her natural abilities blossomed quickly, though it took her quite some time to get published. In the meantime she worked and reworked her manuscripts. Beginning with the publication of *Sense and Sensibility* in 1811, Jane produced a string of novels that exquisitely demonstrate that our struggle to develop good moral character happens on the great battleground we call an ordinary life. After *Sense and Sensibility*, the novels, some of which she had been working on for years, were published in fairly rapid succession: *Pride and Prejudice* (1813), *Mansfield Park* (1814), *Emma* (1815), *Persuasion* (1818), and *Northanger Abbey* (1818). In the entire history of literature, there are few comparable stretches of such fertile literary accomplishment. Though Jane's health began to fail in early 1816 and she wrote less, she was still working on books when she died in 1817. Several of her unfinished manuscripts and early compositions have been published since her death, and her books have remained in print without interruption. Numbered among her countless fans have been such eminent writers as Sir Walter Scott, Henry James, E.M. Forster, Anthony Trollope, G.K. Chesterton, and C.S. Lewis.

Jane's great skill as an author was in uncovering the drama that lay just below the surface niceties of our daily lives—that drama that emerges from romantic longings and entanglements, unspoken emotions, strained relationships, and the struggle between societal expectations and the desires of the individual person. Her novels are neither epic in scope nor filled with adventure. Instead, she chose a small world to write about. It was a world she knew well. She studied it carefully and reproduced it flawlessly. It was a world that stressed the values of virtue, reason, and moderation rather than high-flown sentiment and emotion.

In most of Jane's novels, a key turning point occurs when one of her characters comes to realize that they have not been realistic or correct in their notions of the world or of themselves. The protagonist comes, after many false steps, to the realization that they have seriously misjudged another or treated them unfairly. When this realization happens, it is a moment of genuine spiritual awakening—and encourages repentance from such harmful behaviors. In *Pride and Prejudice*, for example, Elizabeth Bennett comes to realize that she has been blind to the faults of her family, the qualities of her would-be suitor, Mr. Darcy, and the superiority and empty pride within herself:

> *"How despicably I have acted!"* she cried. *"I, who have prided myself on my discernment!...How humiliating is this discovery!...I have courted prepossession and ignorance, and driven reason away...Till this moment I never knew myself."*

Such a moment of self-knowledge serves to initiate positive personal growth.

Jane shows us that it requires great strength to live out a life of moral character in our world, and she reveals this in the most subtle ways. She writes with a tone of gentle irony aimed at our common human character flaws. We often find ourselves laughing at the people in her novels because she is such an on-target observer of human folly. And soon we realize that there is much of ourselves in those at whom we chuckle. She holds up a mirror to our sometimes ridiculous arrogance, desire for status, and unrealistic hopes and expectations. Her biting wit uncovers the many ways we delude ourselves.

Some of Jane's critics are cynical about her stand on faith. Pointing to the lack of attention to religion in the novels and the fact that she often creates clerical characters who are amusing buffoons, critics have suggested that she didn't take her inherited faith all that seriously. Perhaps this is evidence of their own bias more than anything else, for there is plenty of confirmation that this clergyman's daughter was a woman of quiet, but deep faith. While never one to join in with the religious enthusiasts (who made her rather uncomfortable), she was certainly a devout middle-of-the-road Anglican, raised on the spiritual beauty of the *Book of Common Prayer*.

Not only was her father, George Austen, a rector in the Church of England, but two of her brothers also entered the ministry. She also had other relatives who were clergymen. Jane grew up surrounded by an environment where faith could easily be taken for granted. But instead, and by all accounts, she took it very seriously. She attended church services regularly throughout her life and found great enjoyment in reading sermons. On her death, her nephew James Edward Austen-Leigh described her as one who "had lived the life of a good Christian" and that "piety ruled her in life, and supported her in death." He said that she was someone who was more concerned with living out her faith than talking about it.

Although Jane's portrayal of individual clergymen is often not complimentary—witness, for example, the obsequious rector, Mr. Collins, in *Pride and Prejudice*—what she seems to be most critical about is the tendency to treat the ecclesiastical post as a social position more than one of religious duty. She saw the foolishness in self-important clergymen who treated their vocation as though it was just another job, and her characterizations of foolish and narrow-minded vicars are more the result of her respect for faith rather than any sort of disrespect. Jane Austen Scholars have recently discovered, on the back of a page of text from one of her brother's sermons, these words scrawled in her own handwriting: "Men may get in a habit of repeating the words of our Prayers by rote, perhaps without thoroughly understanding—certainly without thoroughly feeling their full force and meaning." For Jane, rote religion was never enough, particularly when it came to prayer.

———◆———

Among the collection of letters and various writings Jane left behind are the prayers presented here. She wrote them to use during evening worship with her family. Couched in a beautiful formality, reminiscent of the *Book of Common Prayer*, they give ample evidence of a woman whose heart and mind were touched by faith. Some of those who knew her best have left written tributes to her memory, and they are all in agreement about several matters: Jane Austen was a gifted writer, a kind and generous woman who often put the needs of others before her own, a person with a quick and delightful wit, and a woman of quiet and sincere reverence toward God.

In her daily life and in her writing, wit and wisdom joined hands with a living faith.